Are you a Snail?

KINGFISHER
LONDON & NEW YORK

Copyright © Macmillan Publishers International Ltd 2000
Text copyright © Judy Allen 2000
Published in the United States by Kingfisher,
120 Broadway, New York, NY 10271
Kingfisher is an imprint of Macmillan Children's Books, London.
All rights reserved.

Distributed in the U.S. and Canada by Macmillan,
120 Broadway, New York, NY 10271

EU representative: Macmillan Publishers Ireland Ltd, 1st Floor, The Liffey Trust Centre, 117-126 Sheriff Street Upper, Dublin 1, D01 YC43

Library of Congress Cataloging-in-Publication Data
Allen, Judy.
Are you a snail?/by Judy Allen; illustrated by Tudor Humphries.–1st ed.
p. cm.– (Backyard Books)
Summary: Introduces the life cycle of a snail, showing how it changes from an egg to an adult snail.
1. Snails–Juvenile literature. 1. Snails. I. Title. II. Series. III. Humphries, Tudor, ill.
QL430.4 . A59 2000
594'.3 21–dc21
99-042382

ISBN: 978-0-7534-5604-0

Kingfisher books are available for special promotions and premiums.
For details contact:
Special Markets Department, Macmillan, 120 Broadway,
New York, NY 10271.
For more information, please visit www.kingfisherbooks.com

Printed in China
19
19TR/0923/DIG(MA)/WKT/128MA

FSC
www.fsc.org
MIX
Paper | Supporting responsible forestry
FSC® C116313

Are you a Snail?

Judy Allen and Tudor Humphries

KINGFISHER
LONDON & NEW YORK

Are you a snail?

If you are, your life began in
an egg like one of these.

When you hatch, you look like this.

This is your mother.

You are much smaller
than your mother.

You are very, very small,
but you will grow.

You have two horns and two eyes on stalks.

You can pull your eyes right down inside the stalks and into your head if you need to.

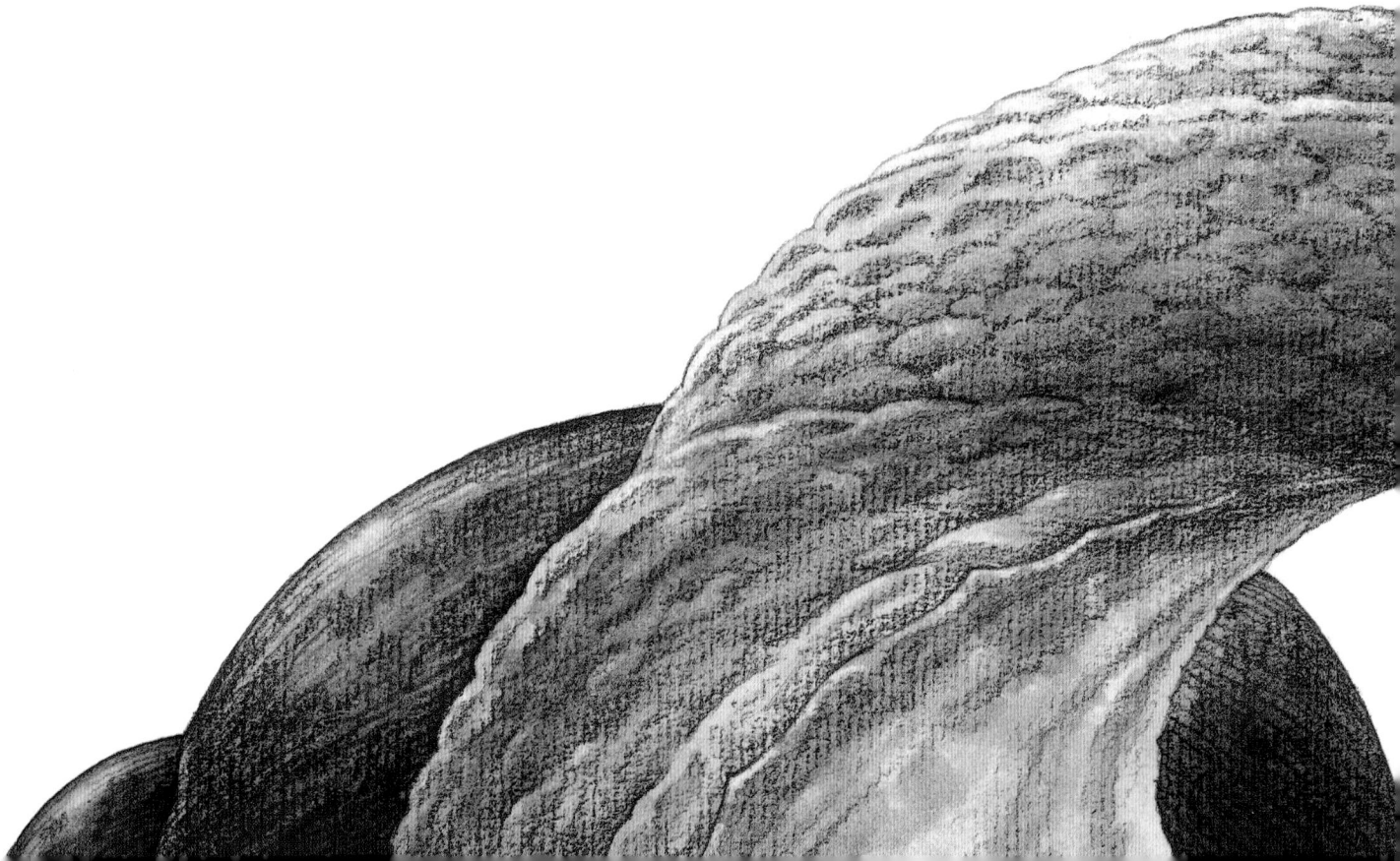

You are slimy. You are VERY slimy.

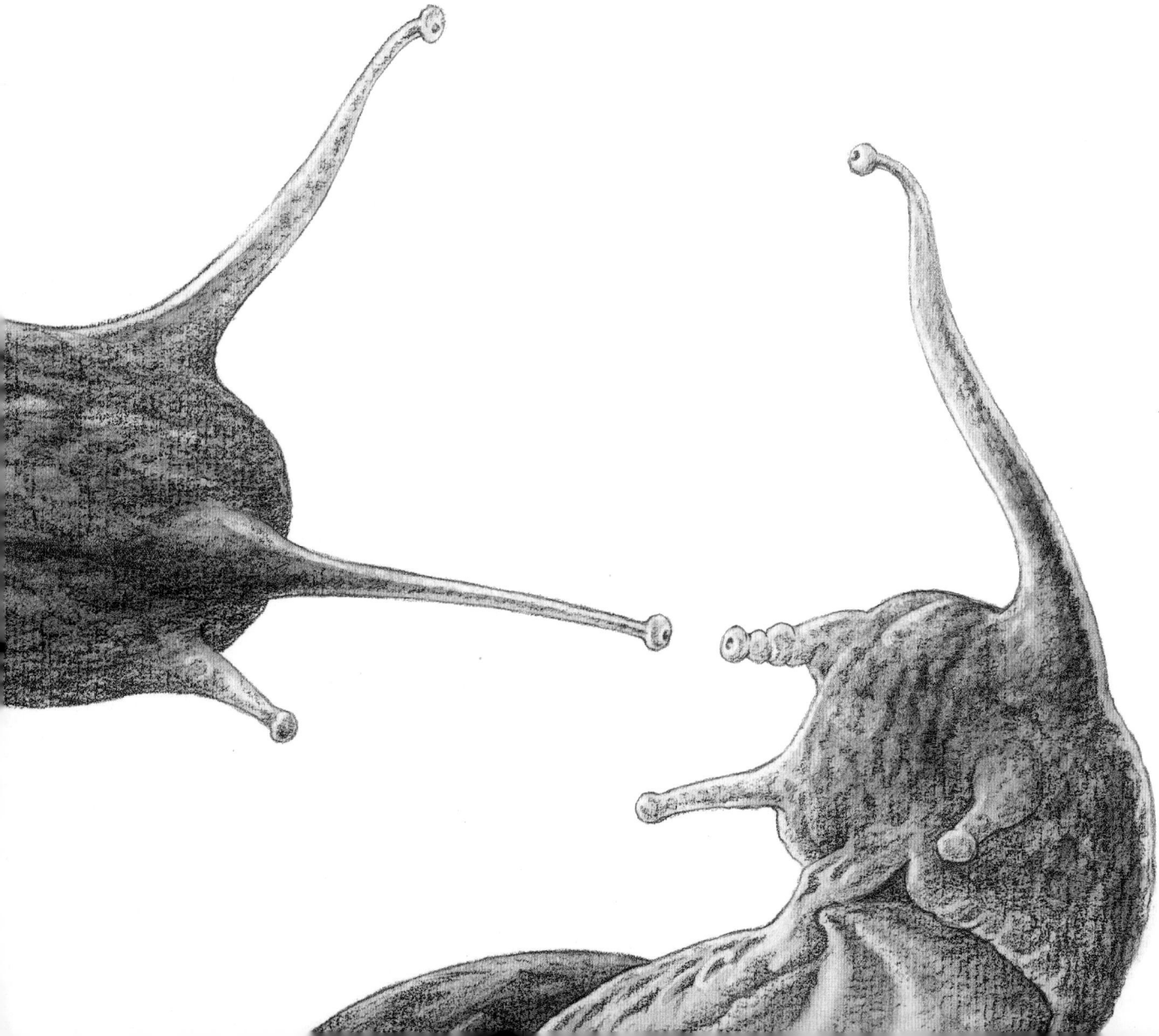

You have a shell
with a beautiful
pattern on it.

You have no
legs and only
one foot, but it
is a strong foot.

The slime on your strong foot
helps you slide along.

Wherever you go, you
leave a silvery, slimy trail.

You like damp places.

You like to be outside
when it has rained.

You have a big, rough tongue
right inside of your mouth.
Use it to rip pieces
off of leaves and
eat them.

Watch out for thrushes.
Thrushes are dangerous.

They like to eat snails.

They know how to break the shells off,
and they don't mind the slime.

Hide in the daytime. Go out at night
when the thrushes are asleep.

Look out for foxes.

Foxes are dangerous.

Hungry foxes eat snails, and they don't mind the slime either.

Foxes go out at night, but you can't hide at night because you need to eat sometime. Just be careful.

Do not go where humans go.
You could get squashed. You move
too slowly to get out of the way.

Humans don't like you because you
eat their plants. They might put poison
or sharp gravel in the garden.

It hurts to walk on gravel.
Also, it sticks to your slime.

And poison? Poison is poisonous!

You may meet someone who looks like this.

It is not a snail whose shell has fallen off. This is a slug.

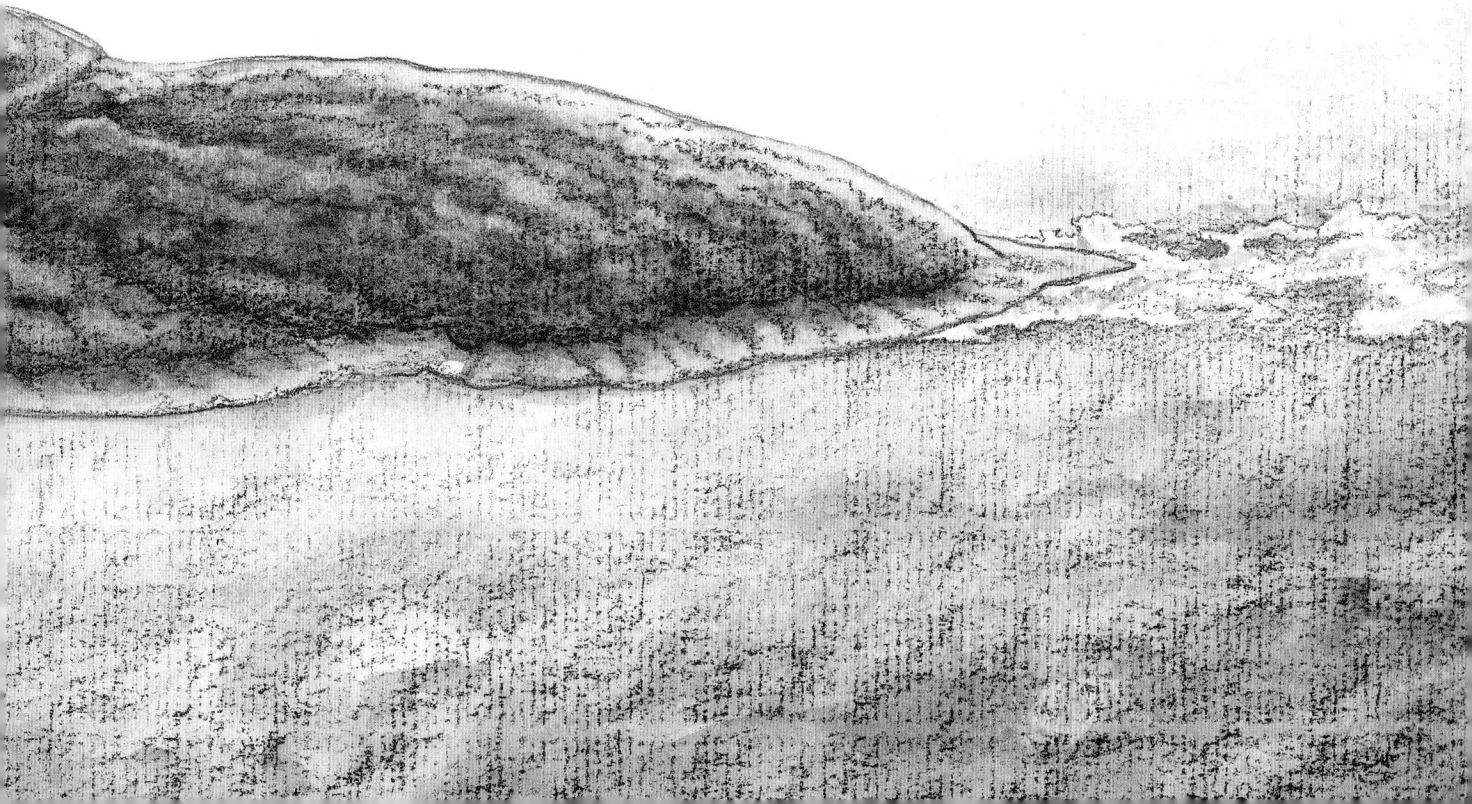

The winter cold makes
you sleepy. Find a safe place.

Your slime hardens into
a door in your shell.

The spring warmth wakes you. Dribble on the inside of your shell door. It melts away.

Slime off and find food.

However, if you look a little

or this

like this

or this

or this

you are
not a snail.

You are . . .

. . . a human child.

You have no shell on your back.
You have no horns and your
eyes are not on stalks.

But you can do a lot of things that snails can't do.

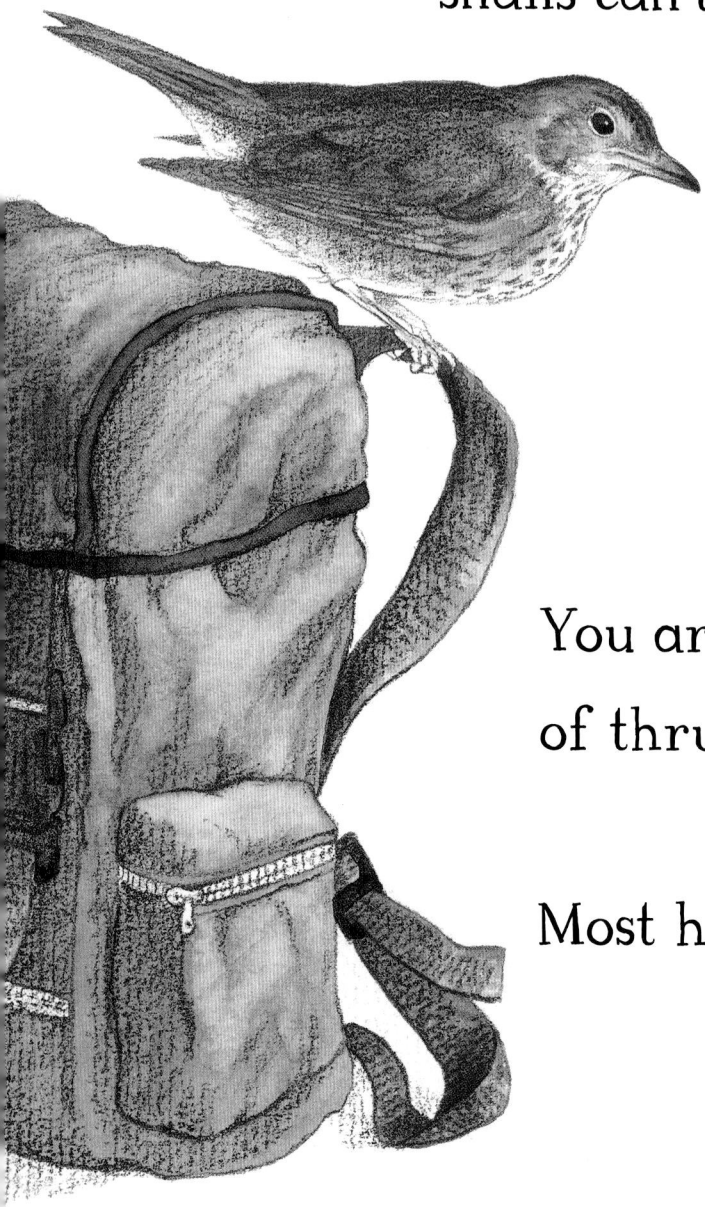

You are not afraid of thrushes or foxes.

Most humans like you.

Best of all, you are not
in the least bit
slimy.

Did You Know . . .

. . . the trail of a snail is broken, but the trail of a slug is one long line of slime.

. . . there are more than 60,000 different kinds of snails.

. . . this is a garden snail, but there are other kinds that live in deserts or swamps, in ponds or rivers, or in the sea.

. . . the Giant African snail can grow very large. The biggest one ever found was almost 16 inches long and weighed two pounds!

. . . snails belong to a family of creatures called gastropods, which means "stomach-foot." So you could say a snail is a stomach on a foot.